Cover Photo: Peregrine falcon chick, Shenandoah National Park, Virginia. Photo by Craig Koppie, U.S. Fish & Wildlife Service.

Monitoring Plan for the American Peregrine Falcon

A Species Recovered Under the Endangered Species Act

December 2003

The Authors
This plan was written by Michael Green, Robert Mesta, Marie Morin, Michael Amaral, Robert Currie, Phil Delphey, Rob Hazlewood, Kathy Hollar, Mary Klee, Angela Matz, Martin Miller, and Ted Swem (Appendix A).

Contact
Address questions about the monitoring plan to Michael Green, National Coordinator, American Peregrine Falcon Monitoring Team, USFWS, Division of Migratory Birds and State Programs, Pacific Region, 911 NE 11th Ave, Portland, OR, 97232. michael_green@fws.gov

Recommended Citation
U.S. Fish and Wildlife Service. 2003. Monitoring Plan for the American Peregrine Falcon, A Species Recovered Under the Endangered Species Act. U.S. Fish and Wildlife Service, Divisions of Endangered Species and Migratory Birds and State Programs, Pacific Region, Portland, OR. 53 pp.

Table of Contents

APPENDICES

LIST OF FIGURES

Acknowledgments

This monitoring plan was developed by the U.S. Fish and Wildlife Service (FWS) in cooperation with State resource agencies, recovery team members, representatives from each FWS Region, the Divisions of Migratory Birds, Endangered Species, and other partners. Comments received on previous drafts strengthened this plan in several ways. In particular, we acknowledge the statistical assistance of Bob Steidl, University of Arizona, Tucson, and the International Association for Fish and Wildlife Agencies for their assistance distributing the plan for review by State resource agencies.

In preparation for writing this plan, monitoring data were solicited from individuals nationwide (Appendix B). The FWS relied heavily on this information in formulating this plan and will continue to rely on this network to achieve its objectives. Post-delisting monitoring will be successful only through the same multi-partner cooperation through which recovery was accomplished.

Background

The recovery of the American Peregrine Falcon (*Falco peregrinus anatum*) (Peregrines) following the species' near total disappearance from much of the United States is a remarkable story of cooperation among private and public institutions. Peregrine populations were at their lowest in the 1960s and early 1970s, when Peregrines were eliminated from the eastern United States and across the Midwest, and reduced to a few hundred pairs at most in the western United States and Mexico. Populations in Canada and Alaska were probably reduced by 70% or more (Kiff 1988, Enderson et al. 1995). The Peregrine was listed as endangered in 1970 under the Endangered Species Conservation Act of 1969, a precursor to the Endangered Species Act (ESA) of 1973 (16 U.S.C. §§ 1537-1544; see Mesta (1999) for a history of listing actions). Recovery plans outlined the goals that were to be reached in four regions of the United States before the Peregrine could be considered recovered (USFWS 1982a, 1982b, 1984, 1991). Due to a ban on the use of DDT and other chlorinated hydrocarbons, and to successful captive breeding, rearing, and release of over 6,000 Peregrines, there are now over 2,000 pairs breeding each year across the United States (White et al. 2002), more than 400 pairs in Canada (U. Banasch, pers. commun. Feb. 7, 2003), and an estimated 170 pairs in Mexico (Enderson et al. 1995); in addition there are probably as many unpaired "floaters" as paired birds across their range (White et al. 2002). As a result of this comeback and because other recovery goals such as estimates of productivity, thicker egg-shells, and reduced levels of contaminants were nearly completely met in all recovery regions, the Peregrine was removed from the FWS List of Threatened and Endangered Species on August 25, 1999 (64 FR 46541, Mesta 1999). Population growth has continued since delisting (FWS, unpubl. data).

A. The Current Situation with Environmental Contaminants

Local and regional data document the continued presence and effects of persistent chemical compounds in North American Peregrines. Many studies have documented the relationship between concentrations of DDE (a metabolite of DDT) and eggshell thinning (Morse 1994, Steidl et al. 1991, Court et al. 1990, Hickey and Anderson 1968). A 20-year monitoring effort in Alaska suggests that mercury is currently at levels in Peregrines that can affect reproduction, and may be increasing over time (Ambrose et al. 2000). In Texas, mercury, selenium and perhaps DDE may be contributing to low productivity of Peregrines in the Big Bend area (Mora et al. 2002). On the Channel Islands in California, analyses of Peregrine eggs yielded notably high organochlorine residues and thin eggshells in the early 1990s, the legacy of offshore DDT disposal during the 1940s; eggs from six other sites in California and Oregon yielded about half the residue levels found in eggs at the Channel Islands (Jarman 1994). On the eastern shore of Virginia and Maryland, eggs collected had slightly elevated levels of DDE, dieldrin, and mercury, which was associated with reproductive problems (U.S. Fish and Wildlife Service 1994). In New Jersey, concentrations of mercury, DDE, and PCBs in Peregrine eggs were theoretically sufficient to impair reproduction, but negative effects on eggshell thickness

1

and productivity were not apparent (U.S. Fish and Wildlife Service and New Jersey Department of Environmental Protection 1997).

In addition, all Peregrines that winter in countries still using DDT and other pesticides may be at risk of accumulating contaminants from their avian prey (Banasch et al. 1992, Johnstone et al. 1996), some of which return to nest in the north and are a potential source of contaminants for both migratory and nonmigratory Peregrines (Fyfe et al. 1990). In spite of these concerns, DDE residues in the blood taken from female Peregrines captured between 1978 and 1994 during spring migration at Padre Island, Texas decreased below levels that would affect reproduction (Henny et al. 1996). The 1997 North American Regional Action Plan, which recommends that the United States, Canada, and Mexico cooperate in a phased reduction in the use and distribution of DDT across the continent, has been very successful in reducing DDT use in Mexico. It is hoped similar progress can be made in other Latin American countries currently using this and other bioaccumulating pesticides (Commission for Environmental Cooperation 2002).

Thus, although Peregrines are still accumulating contaminants from their prey, the levels are currently low enough to allow for successful reproduction and expansion of the population. Nonetheless, the continual introduction of anthropogenic chemicals to the environment far outpaces research on their effects on wildlife. Peregrines, as predators, remain vulnerable to persistent environmental contaminants. In the final delisting rule, we recognized the possible threat that environmental contaminants pose to the sustained recovery of this species and stated we would include a contaminant monitoring component in the post-delisting monitoring plan. This component is found in the Contaminant Monitoring section below.

B. Peregrine Protections Under Other Laws

The delisting of Peregrines from ESA did not affect their protection under the Migratory Bird Treaty Act (MBTA). The FWS has the legal authority and obligation to regulate take of Peregrines under the MBTA. The Secretary of the Interior is authorized and directed to determine if, and by what means, the take of migratory birds is allowed and to adopt suitable regulations permitting and governing the take (16 U.S.C. § 704). The MBTA and its implementing regulations (50 CFR Parts 20 and 21) prohibit take (see regulations for definition of take). Regulations at 50 CFR 21.28 and 21.30 authorize the issuance of permits to take, possess, transport and engage in commerce with raptors for falconry and for propagation. Other regulations authorize the issuance of permits for scientific collecting (50 CFR 21.23), special purposes such as rehabilitation or education (50 CFR 21.27), and depredation (50 CFR 21.41). Permits are issued if certain criteria are met, including a requirement that the issuance will not threaten a wildlife population (50 CFR 13.21(b)(4)). In addition, issuance of raptor propagation permits requires that we consider whether suitable captive stock is available and whether wild stock is needed to enhance the genetic variability of captive stock. Since delisting, there is renewed interest in taking Peregrines for falconry. Thus, in cooperation with State wildlife agencies, the FWS is analyzing the effects on Peregrine populations of taking wild Peregrines for falconry, and developing guidelines for falconry take.

The delisting rule (Mesta 1999) discussed existing protections to Peregrines that continue despite delisting under ESA, such as those offered by the Federal Insecticide, Fungicide, and Rodenticide Act (7 U.S.C. 136) for new and existing pesticide registration and use; the National Forest Management Act (16 U.S.C. 1600); and the Federal Land Management and Policy Act (43 U.S.C. 1701). Peregrines also are protected by State laws, many of which continue to list the species as threatened or endangered. States may have more restrictive laws protecting wildlife than Federal laws, including restrictions on use for falconry (50 CFR 21.29(b)). Peregrines are also protected internationally by the Convention on International Trade in Endangered Species of Wild Fauna and Flora (CITES). This treaty was established to prevent international trade that may be detrimental to the survival of plants and animals. Peregrines were included in Appendix I of CITES on July 1, 1975.

C. The Delisting Monitoring Requirement of ESA

Section 4(g)(1) of the ESA requires that the U.S. Fish and Wildlife Service (FWS),

> *...implement a system in cooperation with the States to monitor effectively for not less than five years the status of all species which have recovered to the point at which the measures provided pursuant to this Act* [the ESA] *are no longer necessary... .*

In keeping with this mandate, the FWS developed this plan in cooperation with State wildlife or natural resource agencies (States), recovery team members, and other cooperators. It has received extensive review by independent experts. A 30-day public comment period was opened with the publication of a Notice of Availability in the Federal Register on July 31, 2001 (66 FR 39523), and again on September 27, 2001 (66 FR 49395). The Federal Register notices and the plan were also posted on the FWS Endangered Species Program's web page (http://endangered.fws.gov). Meanwhile, the FWS continued to collect and compile data from existing monitoring efforts by States to track continued Peregrine recovery after delisting. Monitoring in association with this plan was initiated in 2002 as a limited, pilot program. A revised draft was distributed within the FWS for comment, to monitoring cooperators, and to the International Association for Fish and Wildlife Agencies on November 22, 2002, for their distribution to States for review. On January 13, 2003, this same version was distributed to individuals and organizations who commented on earlier versions. This version of the plan is based on data collected in 2002, from experience gained while administering a nationwide monitoring program in 2002, and on comments by States and other cooperators on earlier versions of the plan. This version of the plan, and FWS responses to comments on earlier versions, are posted on both the FWS Endangered Species web page (http://endangered.fws.gov/recovery/peregrine) and on the Migratory Birds web page (http://migratorybirds.fws.gov). Any revisions and reports will also be available on the web.

While it is the mandate of the FWS to monitor Peregrines for not less than five years after delisting, in cooperation with States, it should be clear from the outset that the FWS itself will collect only a fraction of the data to fulfill that mandate. The successful implementation of this plan relies on a large number of existing Peregrine monitoring efforts designed and implemented by States, other Federal agencies, non-governmental organizations, and individuals. The FWS intends to support and facilitate these existing efforts and to standardize data collection protocols (detailed below) for a randomly selected subset of nesting territories in each region. It will be necessary to initiate new monitoring efforts in only a few states in 2003. The result will be a collaborative network of governmental and non-governmental partners contributing to this nationwide effort. Ultimately, however, the FWS is responsible for the successful implementation of this monitoring plan.

Objective

This cooperative plan is primarily designed to detect declines in territory occupancy, nest success, and productivity in six regions across the United States. Regional data for all population measures will be combined to examine trends nationwide. Territory occupancy, nest success, and productivity all are indices of population health. Estimates of all three indices were very low between 1950 and 1980 when Peregrine populations declined severely, but rebounded during population recovery (Cade et al. 1988, Enderson et al. 1995, Mesta 1999, White et al. 2002).

Data will be collected from a randomly selected subset of Peregrine territories for five sampling periods, at three-year intervals, with full implementation to begin in 2003 and end in 2015. The plan is designed to achieve an 80% probability ($\beta = 0.20$) of detecting a decline of 12.5 percentage points in territory occupancy and nest success after the first sampling occasion with a Type I error rate of 10% ($\alpha = 0.10$; i.e., there is a 10% chance that the data will indicate a declining trend in nest success or territory occupancy greater than 12.5 percentage points when, in fact, there is no such decline occurring). Smaller declines will be detectable over subsequent sampling occasions. Productivity will be measured from the same subset of territories. Rates of productivity typical of expanding or stable populations average between 1.0 and 2.0 young per occupied territory (refs. in White et al. 2002), and most historical and recent productivity estimates fall within that range (Hickey 1942, Mesta 1999). Thus, data from the first two sampling seasons will be compared to this range; trends will be measurable thereafter. The FWS will also request and synthesize population and territory location data collected by States and other partners and report this information with a regional perspective for years that fall in between the monitoring years suggested by this plan. Finally, we will collect addled eggs and feather samples and archive these for later analysis of contaminant levels in

Peregrines nationwide if information indicates that contaminants may be causing a significant population decline.

The FWS will receive data collected by States, other agencies, and partners across the nation, and will analyze these after each monitoring effort; we will propose adjustments to the sampling design if necessary. The plan is designed to detect declines in regional Peregrine populations that might arise from a variety of threats, including but not limited to environmental contaminants and disease (such as West Nile Virus). If these data or other substantial information indicate that this species is experiencing significant regional decreases in territory occupancy, nest success, or productivity, the FWS will initiate more intensive review or studies to determine the cause, and to determine whether or not to relist the species under ESA § 4(b)(7).

Implementation

Region 1 of the FWS has the lead for this monitoring effort. On October 1, 2002, primary lead within the Region transferred from the Division of Endangered Species to the Division of Migratory Birds and State Programs, although the two Divisions will continue to cooperate on implementation of the monitoring plan. A FWS team comprising a National Coordinator and coordinators from each of the FWS Regions (Regional Coordinators) was established to finalize and implement the monitoring plan (Appendix A).

The role of the National Coordinator is to:
- convene the team to finalize and update the monitoring plan, as needed;
- provide guidance to the Regional Coordinators;
- publish the Notice of Availability for the monitoring plan in the Federal Register and on the Endangered Species and Migratory Birds web sites;
- distribute the plan to the FWS Director, Regional Directors, and also to the Assistant Directors for Endangered Species, and Migratory Birds and State Programs, State resource agency directors, and cooperators;
- plan, implement, and analyze the surveys, and summarize monitoring results in cooperation with States and other cooperators;
- prepare interim and final reports;
- organize meetings as necessary to evaluate and plan monitoring efforts with Regional, State, and other cooperators;
- publish a Notice of Availability for the interim and final reports in the Federal Register and on the Endangered Species and Migratory Birds web sites;

- provide copies to the FWS Director, Regional Directors, and also to the Assistant Directors for Endangered Species, and Migratory Birds and State Programs, State resource agency directors, and cooperators;
- make recommendations based on survey results;
- report each year to the FWS Director, Regional Directors, and the Assistant Directors for Endangered Species and Migratory Birds and State Programs, and State resource agency directors on the status of the monitoring plan;
- organize and submit regional budget requests to sources within the FWS;
- seek partnerships with other agencies to implement the plan;
- seek funding opportunities to complete analyses of samples collected for contaminant monitoring.

The role of Regional Coordinators is to:
- establish or maintain a network of cooperators who monitor Peregrines within their FWS Region;
- participate in established regional working group meetings, or establish a regional working group, as necessary, to assist in the planning and implementation of the triennial surveys;
- coordinate with tribes to monitor the randomly selected territories on tribal lands;
- seek partnerships with tribes, governmental agencies and non-governmental organizations within the FWS Region to implement the plan;
- make recommendations to the monitoring team based on survey results;
- coordinate the collection and compilation of regional survey results;
- provide monitoring results to the National Coordinator for inclusion into the interim and final reports by November 1 of the survey year;
- ensure that monitoring data are collected using methods that meet the requirements of this monitoring plan;
- inform tribes, States, and other cooperators which territories have been selected by the random draw for each State;
- determine budget requirements to carry out monitoring in their FWS Region and help secure potential funding from cooperators;
- submit regional funding needs to the National Coordinator, and assist in distributing funds to the cooperators;
- coordinate contaminant monitoring within FWS Regions (ensure that collection protocols are followed, collection activities are properly permitted, and specimens are transferred to the designated archiving facility).

Monitoring already occurs in most states with breeding Peregrines where it is carried out by States, some Federal agencies, private organizations, and many individuals. In only a few areas will new monitoring efforts begin as a result of this monitoring plan. Regional coordinators have been working with, and will continue to work with, all of the cooperators leading these efforts both established and new.

Methods

Territories will be monitored for occupancy, nest success, and productivity in six monitoring regions every three years, starting in 2003 and ending in 2015. Parameter estimates will be compared to values in the scientific literature considered indicative of healthy populations after each sampling period and again at the conclusion of the entire monitoring period.

A. Parameters and Definitions

Data on occupancy, nest success, and productivity will be collected at each territory randomly selected for monitoring. Different States have used different definitions for terms such as "Active" or "Occupied" territories, but for the purposes of this post-delisting monitoring plan, the following definitions will be used:

- Occupied Territory - a territory where either a pair of Peregrines is present (two adults or an adult/subadult mixed pair), or there is evidence of reproduction [e.g., one adult is observed sitting low in the nest, eggs or young are seen, or food is delivered into eyrie (nest site)]. Occupancy for a territory must be established for at least one of two, and possibly more, 4-hour site visits. Occupancy within a region is the number of occupied territories divided by the number of territories that were checked for occupancy.

- Nest Success - the proportion of occupied territories in a monitoring region in which one or more young ≥ 28 days old is observed, with age determined following guidelines in Cade et al. (1996).

- Productivity - the number of young observed at ≥ 28 days old per occupied territory, averaged across a monitoring region.

Typically productivity is determined when nestlings have reached at least 80% of average age of fledging (Steenhof 1987) – 34 days in the case of Peregrines, which fledge about 43 days after hatching. Determining the number of young in a nest with absolute certainty is often difficult unless observers actually visit the eyrie (e.g., when banding young). Thus, for measuring productivity, this plan encourages observers to spend the time necessary to count as many young as possible. This definition of productivity allows that some young might not be observed during the final nest visit, resulting in an underestimate of productivity. Nonetheless, productivity defined in this way remains a more informative index of breeding performance than nest success alone. We will continue to use all three measures, territory occupancy, nest success, and productivity to assess population health.

Cade et al. (1996) recommend banding nestling Peregrines at 21 to 35 days old; older nestlings are more likely to scramble away and potentially be injured or killed in the process, and younger chicks are difficult to differentiate by sex. The 28-day minimum nestling age we have set to determine nest success and productivity allows banders about six days in which to band nestlings and contribute productivity data. If workers band birds before day 28, an additional visit on or after day 28 would be necessary to count nestlings for this parameter. We acknowledge that some nestling mortality occurs between 28 days of age and fledging; for this reason, both measures of breeding success may be overestimates (Steenhof 1987).

The sample data form in Appendix C includes the minimum data requested for this monitoring effort.

B. Monitoring Regions

The six monitoring regions in this plan follow FWS Region boundaries, but combine FWS Region 3 in the Midwest and Region 5 in the Northeast. These monitoring regions are similar to the original four recovery regions, except that the Rocky Mountain/Southwest recovery region is split into FWS Regions 2 and 6, and the Eastern recovery region is split by FWS Region 4 (Figure 1 and Appendix D). We made additional boundary adjustments to the original recovery regions to align monitoring regions with FWS Regions, particularly in Great Plains states, where there are few known breeding Peregrines. Since the recovery of Peregrines was based upon reaching recovery goals in designated recovery regions, it seemed prudent to monitor population trends at the same, or finer, geographic scale. Splitting the original recovery regions into the smaller FWS Regions reflects local and regional concerns within those FWS Regions, and administrative convenience. Administratively, the responsibility for implementing this monitoring plan will be from within FWS Regions working closely with States and other cooperators.

The monitoring regions follow:

- Pacific (FWS Region 1): CA, ID, NV, OR, WA;
- Southwestern (FWS Region 2): AZ, NM, TX, and OK;
- Rocky Mountain/Great Plains (FWS Region 6): CO, KS, MT, ND, NE, SD, UT, WY;
- Midwestern/Northeastern (FWS Regions 3 and 5): IL, IN, IA, MI, MN, MO, OH, WI, CT, DE, ME, MD, MA, NH, NJ, NY, PA, RI, VT, VA;
- Southeastern (FWS Region 4): GA, KY, NC, SC, TN; and
- Interior Alaska (FWS Region 7): AK.

C. Frequency and Duration of Sampling

The Monitoring Team chose to monitor Peregrines five times at three-year intervals, beginning in 2003 and ending in 2015 (i.e., sampling will occur in 2003, 2006, 2009, 2012, and 2015). Five monitoring periods meets the requirement of ESA (to monitor "...for not less than five years..."); the three-year interval spreads the monitoring over 13 years, reflecting our concern for the long-term future of the Peregrine.

The Peregrine population currently is secure; the population continues to increase as it has for 30 years (Figure 2). The Monitoring Team believes this trend will continue at least over the short-term. The long-term future is less certain; although the threat to Peregrines from some contaminants has been controlled, we believe that contaminants still pose the most likely future threat to Peregrine populations. They have a demonstrated vulnerability to contaminants, exposure to contaminants still occurs, and future compounds might pose a risk to Peregrines (see *The Current Situation with Environmental Contaminants*, above). Population-level effects from contaminants are likely to take place over a relatively long- rather than short-term. Monitoring every year over the long-term would be unnecessary in the face of increasing population trends and it would be costly. In the end, monitoring 5 times at 3 year intervals over 13 years will provide sufficient comparative data and trend information on territory occupancy, nest success and productivity to measure effects from what we believe to be the most likely potential threats to Peregrines, contaminants.

At the end of the 13-year monitoring plan the FWS will review all available information to determine if continuation of monitoring is appropriate (see Reports, below). As a point of reference, Canada has been monitoring nest site occupancy and productivity of Peregrines every five years since 1970 and populations continue to expand in Canada as in the United States (Rowell et al. 2003).

D. Sample Size

The minimum number of territories to sample per monitoring region is based on territory occupancy and nest success data collected mainly over the past four years (1999-2002) from Peregrine territories across the nation (Appendix E). These data were collected separately by Regional Coordinators from their networks of cooperators. Nationwide, the occupancy rate for territories occupied at least once since 1999 was 84%, ranging from an average of 75% to 94% among regions (Appendix F). For occupied territories, nest success was 68% nationwide (61% - 73%, Appendix F). These estimates of territory occupancy and nest success compare well with rates estimated for populations thought to be healthy (70-90% for territory occupancy, 45-66% for nest success, summarizing pre-1955 or post-1985 data from Hickey and Anderson 1969, Enderson and Craig 1974, and Ratcliffe 1993). In contrast, when Peregrine populations were in serious decline during the 1950s and 1960s, rates of territory occupancy and nest success were at or near zero in some regions. For example, it was believed that not a single Peregrine fledged in the northeast United States in 1962 (Hickey and Anderson 1969). Further, the once healthy

9

Hudson River population ceased reproducing by 1950 and most sites were unoccupied by the mid-1950s (Herbert and Herbert 1969). By 1965 only 33% of known territories in the Rocky Mountains remained occupied (Enderson 1969). In Canada and Alaska, territory occupancy was 50% or less in the 1970s (Enderson et al. 1995). Ratcliffe (1993) demonstrated a similar decline in nest success and territory occupancy in Great Britain during in the 1960s and 1970s, as well as recovery since 1980.

Estimates of nest success from 1999-2002 (68%) and from the period of population decline provide upper and lower limits within which we would expect North American Peregrines to perform. Because the nationwide estimate of nest success, 68%, is lower than territory occupancy, 84%, and was similar across the seven FWS Regions (61% - 73%, Appendix F), we used this estimate of nest success to establish sample sizes for each monitoring region. Considering historical and current rates, we decided that if nest success declined to 55% or less (a drop of 13 percentage points), there would be cause for concern in the short-term.

To establish sample sizes, we chose a decline of 12.5 percentage points as a short-term monitoring target to represent a potential decline from 68% to 55%. We established the rate at which we are willing to accept Type II errors (β) at 20% (or equivalently, power = 80%) and the rate at which we are willing to accept Type I errors (α) at 10%[1]. Using these constants, we determined that 72 occupied territories per monitoring region would need to be checked to detect a drop of 12.5 percentage points or more in nest success from current levels (i.e., 68%) with 80% power. We know, however, that on average, 75% or more territories are occupied in any given year [the range among regional averages is 75% (Region 2) to 94% (Region 7) Appendix F]; thus to achieve a sample size of 72 occupied territories, we need to check 96 territories in each region (72 ÷ 0.75). (Average territory occupancy in Region 2 varied between 67% and 80% from 1999 through 2002, but these data are considered underestimates for several reasons; thus we determined that a sample size calculated from the average, rather than the minimum territory occupancy estimate in Region 2, was a reasonable approach.) This sample size will allow somewhat greater power to detect a drop of 12.5 percentage points or more in territory occupancy than it will for nest success.

The minimum sample size of 96 territories per monitoring region applies to four of the six monitoring regions. The Southeastern monitoring region has only 18 known

---

[1] — We considered the practical and biological implications of various levels of Type 1 (α) and Type 2 (β) errors, and of the magnitudes of declines we wished to detect establishing numbers of territories to monitor. The 55% nest success target is lower than expected of healthy populations, higher than that of populations during their declines in DDT years, and similar to that of a recovering population in southeastern Arizona (58%; Ellis 1988). The team thus decided that if nest success declined to 55% we would be concerned, and some management action should be initiated. A strategy recommended when designing monitoring programs for species of conservation interest is to minimize β (the chance of missing a decline) versus α (the chance of wrongly determining a decline is occurring) (Steidl et al. 1997). The monitoring team decided that β = 20% and α = 10% were reasonable levels for monitoring at the regional scale, understanding that β will be smaller (and power higher) if actual declines in these parameters are higher than rates established. Further, when data from regions are combined for analysis, power will be higher, and thus the ability to detect smaller declines in nest success will increase.

territories, and all will be monitored. Therefore, noting declines in population parameters in this region is not as dependent on sampling because all territories, rather than some proportion, will be monitored each monitoring year. FWS Region 7 will continue to monitor Peregrines along portions of both the Tanana and Yukon rivers as an index of regional population trends; the study area contained 92 territories in 2002. Similarly, all Peregrine territories are currently being monitored in the Midwestern/Northeastern region, so territories randomly selected for this plan are a subset of what is actually being monitored in this region. Summing all monitoring regions, the minimum number of territories sampled across the nation will be about 494 in 2003.

E. Analyses

Territory occupancy and nest success data will be compared to the regional and nationwide estimates from 1999 to 2002; territory occupancy nationwide was estimated at 84% and ranged from 75% to 94%, and nest success nationwide was estimated at 68% and ranged from 61% to 73% (Appendix F). Declines from sample estimates and these target values greater than 13 percentage points will trigger a response by the FWS (see the Data Evaluation - *Response Triggers* section, below). Additionally, to determine whether or not the estimated sample percentages for nest success and occupancy are unusual compared to the target values of each, instead of performing a statistical test we will instead calculate a 90% confidence interval on each estimated sample percentage (Steidl et al. 1997). If the regional or nationwide target value is included within the confidence interval, we will conclude the observed proportion is within normal range and take no action. If the upper confidence bound falls below the target value, we will conclude the observed proportion is lower than normal, and take some action (see the Data Evaluation - *Response Triggers* section, below).

Productivity data will be compared to recent state and local estimates, as well as to historical rates. Recent productivity data from recovery regions in the United States ranged from 1.2 to 1.9 young per territorial pair (Mesta 1999). Historical rates of productivity for various regions of the United States range from 0.7 to 1.5 young per occupied site (Hickey 1942). Productivity reported during the period of decline was near zero (Hickey and Anderson 1969, Enderson and Craig 1974). Ratcliffe (1993) suggests that when productivity drops to ≤ 0.8 young per pair and remains low for several years, reproduction is low enough to affect recruitment into the breeding population. Hunt (1998) modeled population dynamics of Peregrines under various rates of adult mortality and juvenile survival. Peregrine populations are at least stable when productivity is from 1.0 to 2.0 young per pair, adult mortality is $< 15\%$ and juvenile mortality is $< 70\%$; these productivity figures are consistent with estimates in expanding or stable populations in the United States (Corser et al. 1999, Mesta 1999, Hayes and Buchanan 2002). Regional or national estimates of productivity that fall below 1.0 young per pair will initiate a special review (see the Data Evaluation - *Response Triggers* section, below).

After the completion of three sampling periods (in 2009), we will be able to expand the analyses to include trends in rates of territory occupancy, nest success, and productivity.

Additional analyses might also be appropriate. For example, regional data might be combined to examine rates and trends for the entire nation. With a nationwide sample of 494 territories, an analysis of territory occupancy and nest success will have greater statistical power to detect smaller declines at the national level than is possible at the regional level.

Nationwide, the random selection of territories will include both territories with eyries on manmade structures and on natural features; to the extent allowed by the data we will evaluate the implications of these differences in nest location on territory occupancy, nest success, and productivity. If an analysis of the data show declining trends or cause for concern, then the FWS, States and other cooperators will evaluate why this might be the case (see the Data Evaluation - *Response Triggers* section, below).

F. Territory Selection

In 2003 the monitoring team selected territories randomly from the pool of territories within a monitoring region known to have been occupied at least once from 1999 through 2002 (during or after the delisting year 1999). (Data from 1997 contributed to the pool for Arizona, which lacks more recent data.) The Regional Coordinators obtained these data from a variety of cooperators. The FWS did not request and does not have geographic coordinates for these territories; specific location information is maintained separately by States and other partners.

Territories monitored after 2003 (i.e., in 2006, 2009, 2012, and 2015) will either be all of the same randomly chosen territories from 2003, a new randomly chosen set, or a mixture of the two (as recommended in the Mexican Spotted Owl recovery plan, USFWS 1995). Monitoring the same set of territories each sampling year would add efficiency and reduce bias as monitors become more familiar with the selected territories over time. Following the 2003 season and after initial data analyses, the monitoring team, working in cooperation with States, will propose a method for selecting territories to monitor in 2006 and all subsequent sampling years.

The Southeastern and Interior Alaska monitoring regions are special cases. The numbers of territories are so few, and the level of interest and cooperation so high in the Southeastern region, that the FWS, other Federal agencies, States, and cooperators will monitor all known territories to the extent possible (18 active territories known as of 2002). In Alaska, the current monitoring effort is a count along stretches of two rivers (Ambrose and Riddle 1988); this sample is used as an index of the larger population (ca. 1,000 breeding pairs) in a region where most sites are remote and ground access to eyries is a challenge.

In four monitoring regions, the following minimum number of territories were randomly selected. In the Interior Alaska monitoring region, the sample comprises territories along 2 river systems, and in the Southeast monitoring region the entire population is monitored:

- Pacific: 96 territories;
- Southwestern: 96 territories;
- Rocky Mountains: 96 territories;
- Midwestern/Northeastern: 96 territories;
- Southeastern: 18 territories (in 2002); and
- Interior Alaska: a sample of territories along stretches of 2 rivers (48 on the Yukon and 44 on the Tanana rivers in 2002).

G. Monitoring Protocol

During each sampling iteration, each randomly selected territory will be visited two or more times to determine occupancy, nest success, and productivity. Visits to the territory will be timed appropriately for the geographic areas. The first visit will occur during late courtship, egg laying, or early incubation to determine occupancy; a second visit will occur during the early nestling stage to determine the age of the nests, or to check the 'unoccupied' status of territories still in question; and a third visit (or more) will be made to occupied territories during the late nestling stage, when young are 28-42 days old to determine nest success and productivity. Even if no evidence of territory occupancy is found in the first four hour visit, a second visit of four hours (ideally three to four weeks later) is required for the territory to be deemed unoccupied. During all visits, the number and age (adult or subadult) of Peregrines seen in the territory should be recorded, with behavioral or physical evidence of breeding activity if observed. Peregrines sometimes have alternate nest sites within a single territory. If the territory checked does not appear to be occupied, some realistic survey effort should be expended to try and locate potential alternate nest sites within the territory.

Nest monitoring will be done during favorable weather conditions by observers familiar with Peregrine nesting behavior. Observers should avoid flushing incubating Peregrines, and should not monitor during poor weather (e.g., heavy rain, snow, high winds), when disturbance of incubation could alter the outcome of the nest. If possible, observations should occur when Peregrines are likely to be most active; in some areas this is just prior to dark or at first light (Fuller and Mosher 1987). Observers must minimize stress to the Peregrines caused by their presence, and observation posts, in general, should be far enough from the nest so as to not elicit sustained territorial behavior from either adult [150 - 1700 meters is recommended (Pagel 1992), although closer approach might be tolerated by some pairs, particularly in urban settings]. Observers must have appropriate equipment, such as good binoculars, a high quality portable spotting scope, or both. Chick age can be determined by reference to Cade et al. (1996; available through The Peregrine Fund); this reference has a great deal of additional, helpful survey techniques and recommendations. Field notebooks are recommended for detailed field notes. The minimum information to be recorded is on the Sample Data Form, Appendix C. Regional working groups should convene before the monitoring program is initiated to develop a standard logistical protocol for collecting survey data within their monitoring region, if necessary. Data collected should be forwarded to the Regional Coordinator for that region.

States, FWS Regions, and private programs are encouraged to continue to monitor all known Peregrine nesting territories if they are doing so already, and not limit their monitoring to the randomly selected territories as in this plan. Many States, some Federal agencies, and other partners annually monitor occupancy, nest success, and productivity, and they conduct searches for new territories, band and color-mark chicks, collect prey remains and unhatched eggs, and trap adults. Through Regional Coordinators, the FWS National Coordinator will request population data collected and new territory locations found in years that fall between the monitoring years described in this plan. The FWS will synthesize these data and report this information with a regional perspective for years that fall between the monitoring years suggested in this plan. We also anticipate that some States will contribute or conduct other research. These efforts are encouraged, as they will contribute to our understanding of the population status of Peregrines.

Peregrine Status and Monitoring in Canada

The Canadian Wildlife Service coordinates a national Peregrine population survey once every five years and will conduct three surveys (2005, 2010 and 2015) during the 12-year monitoring period. Observers in Canada make one or two visits to known territories to determine territory occupancy and, if possible, productivity data. In remote locations in some Provinces territories are monitored by helicopter, and only once per season. These visits are timed to coincide with the nestling stage so a count of nestlings can be made. Observers are encouraged to note additional potential habitat and territories while in the field for future monitoring. The breeding population in Canada is now estimated at over 400 pairs (U. Banasch, pers. commun Feb. 7, 2003). The results of these national surveys will be considered when evaluating the status of Peregrines in North America.

Peregrine Status and Monitoring in Mexico

There are no systematic surveys of Peregrines in Mexico. Mesta (1999) summarizes what little information exists on the current status of the species breeding south of the United States border. Local data suggest some populations underwent similar declines and are recovering as in the United States and Canada. Enderson et al. (1995) estimated 170 pairs nest in Mexico. Contaminants are more of a concern in Mexico than in the United States. As a result of tri-national agreements Mexico is phasing out the use of DDT, but use of this and other persistent organic pollutants continues in other Latin American countries (Commission for Environmental Cooperation 2002); contaminants continue to be a concern for Peregrines breeding south of the United States border and for others migrating through countries that continue to use bio-accumulating contaminants.

Contaminant Monitoring

The scientific community widely accepts that exposure to environmental contaminants was the single factor that caused the near extirpation of Peregrines from North America, and restrictions on the use of persistent organochlorine compounds in the United States and Canada allowed Peregrines and other predatory birds to recover. As a result, recovery goals in two regions included measures of eggshell thickness; in one of these (Alaska), recovery goals also included contaminant loads in eggs (Mesta 1999).

In spite of restrictions on their use, Peregrines continue to accumulate persistent organochlorine pesticides and other compounds, both domestically and in countries through which they migrate or winter (see above, *The Current Situation with Environmental Contaminants*). Further, the continual introduction of anthropogenic chemicals to the environment requires vigilance and monitoring of vulnerable wildlife, especially predators at the top of the food chain such as Peregrines.

This section provides a plan for monitoring loads of past, current, or emerging contaminants of concern in Peregrines. Samples will be collected in conjunction with population monitoring as described below and in Appendix G. Federal and State permits are required to collect samples. Contact FWS Regional Coordinators for more information.

We believe that monitoring territory occupancy, nest success, and productivity will adequately achieve the objectives of ESA requirements for post-delisting monitoring. However, we are including a contaminants monitoring component to develop a contaminants record that will be available for analysis if information indicates that contaminants may be implicated in a significant population decline. Nonetheless, we will continue to seek funds for contemporary analysis, regardless of whether or not a population decline occurs.

A. Egg Samples

A variety of sample types have been used for contaminants monitoring. Eggs can be analyzed for at least two major classes of contaminants: persistent organic pollutants such as DDT and its metabolite DDE, other organochlorine pesticides, polychlorinated biphenyls (PCBs), and dioxins; and heavy metals such as cadmium and mercury. When combined with adequate productivity data, egg contaminants data can be used to assess population-level reproductive effects. Eggshell thickness, which was affected by DDE, is routinely measured on eggs collected for contaminants. Thickness data are compared to pre-DDT era thickness from museum specimens or other reference populations, and can be correlated with DDE levels in the sampled eggs.

Eggs can be collected opportunistically during nest visits, either as "fresh" eggs during incubation or as unhatched "addled" eggs during the nestling stage. At this time, only addled eggs will be collected for monitoring, to avoid removing potentially viable eggs. Regardless of timing of collection, embryo development will be noted for all eggs collected (among other data, including egg shell thickness; Appendix G).

B. Feather Samples

Metals and organic contaminants can be measured in blood, but in general the sample volumes required and the relatively invasive technique preclude widespread use of this matrix. Feathers (excluding natal down) can be analyzed for metals. With consistent collection (identical feathers from same-age Peregrines), nestling feathers (excluding natal down) reflect natal area contaminant exposure. Therefore, regional projects which include nest visits for banding purposes should also include collection of nestling feathers.

To collect feathers, the largest nestling (which is often the nestling with the most advanced feather development) will be the only nestling sampled per nest. Up to 1.5 cm of the distal part of the 4th secondary wing feather, from one side only, will be removed using clean stainless steel scissors. Care must be taken to not cut the follicle, which is vascularized, and therefore prone to bleeding, during feather development. The sample will be stored in polyethylene collection envelopes such as Whirlpak® envelopes, then transferred to a central storage facility. Collectors will fill out standardized data forms, which will include the date, collector, nest identification and location (latitude and longitude or UTM), the band number, and whether the sample was collected from the left or right side of the nestling.

C. Sample Size

Based on comprehensive monitoring in Alaska (Ambrose et al. 2000), an adequate sample size and interval for samples is 15-20 (addled eggs or feathers) collected over a period of no more than five years. Because the number of available samples may be variable and low in any one year, both sample types should always be collected opportunistically by States and others engaged in permitted activities requiring nest visits (such as banding nestlings), but, at a minimum, samples should be collected in every monitoring region in every monitoring year. Samples will be archived at the central storage facility (Appendix G).

Regional Coordinators are responsible for coordinating collection of a minimum of 20 addled eggs and 20 clipped feathers from nestlings of banding age by September 2009 (the end of the third population monitoring year), and again by September 2015 (the end of the monitoring period). Regional coordinators will also ensure that collection protocols are followed and that collection activities are properly permitted, provide interstate coordination within regions, and coordinate transfer of specimens to a central location. Regions or States already engaged in contaminants analyses are encouraged to coordinate their activities and match protocols. The plan recognizes that some regions may find it difficult to meet minimum sample sizes due to low numbers of nesting pairs, but each region should strive to meet collection goals.

D. Funding and Analyses

Samples will be chemically analyzed contingent upon funding. Efforts to fully fund contaminants analyses will occur regardless of the results of the population monitoring efforts. Negative trends or significant drops in regional or national population indices will initiate a considerably more pointed effort to find funding, and stimulate more funding opportunities. Regardless, funding procurement will require additional coordination among FWS Regional Coordinators, FWS Environmental Contaminants Specialists, States, and other cooperators. When funding is secured, eggs will be analyzed at a minimum for metals and organochlorines, and feathers for metals, according to contractual specifications developed by the FWS Environmental Quality Division in conjunction with chemists at the Patuxent Analytical Control Facility (PACF). Current lists (and costs at FWS contract laboratories) are available through PACF (http://www.pwrc.usgs.gov/pacf/).

Levels of contaminant loading will be compared to measures of reproductive performance at national and regional scales and to published data or thresholds (e.g., as in Peakall et al. 1990), and contaminant loading levels will be analyzed for regional and national trends and variation, with specific analyses dependent upon sample sizes (regional and national) and levels of contamination. Additional chemical or biological analyses may be pursued based upon regional or emerging contaminant concerns.

Data Evaluation

A. Review of Monitoring Data Relative to 'Response Triggers'

The FWS, in cooperation with the States, will evaluate the monitoring results to determine whether or not the results suggest that a more detailed analysis of the status of Peregrines, the monitoring protocol, or both, is necessary. After each triennial monitoring year, Regional Coordinators will work with the States to compile the monitoring results for their respective monitoring region, evaluate the results, and prepare a written assessment. This assessment will include a summary of the monitoring data, state whether any of the parameters fell below the "response triggers" shown below, determine whether or not the data collection protocols are functioning as anticipated and whether or not any changes are needed, and include an initial determination of any threats that may warrant further evaluation by the national monitoring team. In addition, the FWS will analyze and summarize regional data it receives from States and other cooperators in the years between formal surveys.

17

After completion of these triennial (or more frequent) assessments for each monitoring region, the national monitoring team will convene to review the assessments. At that time, the national team will determine whether any action is necessary to respond to the 'triggers' described below and to review any other significant issues raised by the FWS or States in the regional summaries. In response to any significant issues, the national team would consult with regional or national experts to:

- increase the sensitivity of the sampling protocol to detect national or regional declines in any of the parameters by, for example, increasing sample sizes;
- design research that would determine causes of low parameter values or declines in productivity;
- work with States, tribes, or other entities to exercise their regulatory authorities to alleviate known or suspected threats;
- conduct regional or national status assessment(s) to evaluate the significance of threats to Peregrines;
- evaluate proposing Peregrines for relisting under the ESA; or,
- evaluate whether or not to list Peregrines under the emergency provisions of the ESA.

The "response triggers" shown below would not automatically prompt a proposal to relist Peregrines under the ESA, because not all declines in population parameters or declines in productivity would indicate that listing under the ESA would be warranted. Weather, for example, might cause temporary declines in either territory occupancy, nest success, productivity, or all of these parameters over an entire region, and in more than one monitoring season. Also, it is possible that there might be a natural reduction in overall rates of occupancy, nest success, and productivity as regional populations reach carrying capacity. For example, some territories produce more young and are more often occupied than others (refs. in White et al. 2002). After prime locations are taken, less productive and less consistently occupied sites remain. Increased use of these marginal nesting territories due to an increased number of breeding Peregrines might reduce mean nest success and productivity. Should declines be noted, natural causes such as these will be evaluated as well as factors that might threaten or endanger Peregrines. Any relisting decision would be made by evaluating the status of Peregrines relative to the ESA's five listing factors [ESA § 4(a)(1)].

B. Response Triggers

These "response triggers" will, in addition to other factors described above, prompt an evaluation and appropriate response by the national monitoring team, in consultation with national or regional experts, as necessary. The national team will evaluate these triggers within each monitoring region and for all regions combined after each triennial monitoring year:

- 90% confidence intervals around estimated proportions of territory occupancy and nest success, fall below regional and national estimates (Appendix F);
- nest success or territory occupancy has declined by more than 13 percentage points from the average of previous monitoring years;
- average productivity is less than 1.0.

Reports

The FWS will issue a triennial report with data summaries and analyses after each monitoring season; these will be available in printed form and on the world wide web by March of the year following surveys. Reports will also suggest ways to improve sampling protocols or other aspects of the plan design if necessary.

Each report will also comment on the status of Peregrines relative to the need for possible relisting. This plan has been devised to allow early detection of substantial declines in territory occupancy, nest success, and productivity with reasonable certainty and precision. Statistical power to detect smaller declines in these rates will increase with successive monitoring seasons, as data from these seasons will likely be combined into larger sample sizes. Regardless, if declines in territory occupancy, nest success, or productivity become large enough to cause concern in monitoring regions or nationwide, then the monitoring team will convene, consult with regional working groups, States and other partners, and make recommendations for future action to the FWS Region 1 Divisions of Endangered Species, and Migratory Birds and State Programs (see the Data Evaluation - *Response Triggers* section, above).

Reports might also be produced between years, as the FWS will annually request data collected by States and cooperators, for regional analyses of population health. At the very least, these data will be summarized in the triennial report.

At the end of the 13-year monitoring period, the FWS will review all available information to determine if continuation of monitoring is appropriate. The decision to continue or end the monitoring program will be explained in the final monitoring report, which will be published in the Federal Register. If the Peregrine population is stable range-wide and no significant threats are identified, then monitoring may be terminated, or a different monitoring program might be developed with cooperators.

Funding

Post-delisting monitoring is a cooperative effort between the FWS; State, tribal, and foreign governments; other Federal agencies; and other non-governmental partners under the ESA. Funding of post-delisting monitoring presents a challenge for all the partners committed to ensuring the continued viability of Peregrines following the removal of ESA protections. To the extent feasible, the FWS intends to provide funding for post-delisting monitoring efforts from annual Endangered Species general Recovery Program appropriations. Nonetheless, nothing in this plan should be construed as a commitment or requirement that any Federal agency obligate or pay funds in contravention of the Anti-Deficiency Act (31 U.S.C. § 1341) or any other law or regulation.

Literature Cited

Ambrose, R.E., A. Matz, T. Swem, and P. Bente. 2000. Environmental contaminants in American and arctic peregrine falcon eggs in Alaska, 1979-95. Technical Report NAES-TR-00-02, U.S. Fish and Wildlife Service, Northern Alaska Ecological Services, Fairbanks, AK. 67 pp.

Ambrose, R.E. and K.E. Riddle. 1988. Population dispersal, turnover, and migration of Alaska peregrines. Pp 677-684 *In* Peregrine falcon populations: their management and recovery. T.J. Cade, J.H. Enderson, C.G Thelander, and C.M. White, eds. The Peregrine Fund, Boise, Idaho.

Banasch, U., J.P. Goossen, A.E. Riez, C. Casler, and R.D. Barradas. 1992. Organochlorine contaminants in migrant and resident prey of peregrine falcons, *Falco peregrinus*, in Panama, Venezuela, and Mexico. Can. Field-Nat. 106:493-498.

Bird, D.M, J. Gautier, and V. Montpetit. 1984. Embryonic growth of American kestrels. Auk 101:392-396.

Cade, T.J., J.H. Enderson, C.G Thelander, and C.M. White, eds. 1988. Peregrine falcon populations: their management and recovery. The Peregrine Fund, Boise, Idaho.

Cade, T.J., J.H. Enders, and J. Linthicum. 1996. Guide to management of Peregrine Falcons at the eyrie. The Peregrine Fund, Boise, Idaho.

Commission for Environmental Cooperation. 2002. Report on the activities of the Commission for Environmental Cooperation. Montreal, Canada, Fall 2002. http://www.cec.org/files/pdf/PUBLICATIONS/rptfall2002e

Corser, J.D., M. Amaral, C.J. Martin, and C.C. Rimmer. 1999. Recovery of a cliff-nesting Peregrine Falcon, *Falco peregrinus*, population in northern New York and New England, 1984-1996. Can. Field- Nat. 113:472-480.

Court, G.S., C.C. Gates, D.A. Boag, J.D. MacNeil, D.M. Bradley, A.C. Fesser, J.R. Patterson, G.B. Stenhouse, and L.W. Oliphant. 1990. A toxicological assessment of peregrine falcons, *Falco peregrinus tundrius*, breeding in the Keewatin District of the Northwest Territories, Canada. Can. Field-Nat. 104:255-272.

Custer, T.W., G.W. Pendleton, and R.W. Roach. 1992. Determination of hatching date for eggs of black-crowned night-heron, snowy egrets, and great egrets. J. Field. Ornithol. 63:145-154.

Ehrlich, P.R., D.S. Dobkin, and D. Wheye. 1988. The Birder's Handbook. Simon and Schuster, Inc., New York, NY, USA. 785 pp.

Ellis, D.H. 1988. Distribution, productivity, and status of the Peregrine Falcon in Arizona. Pp 87-94 *In* Peregrine falcon populations: their management and recovery. T.J. Cade, J.H. Enderson, C.G Thelander, and C.M. White, eds. The Peregrine Fund, Boise, Idaho.

Enderson, J.H. 1969. Population trends among Peregrine Falcons in the Rocky Mountain region. Pp. 73-79 *In* Peregrine Falcon populations: their biology and decline. J.J. Hickey, ed. Univ. of Wisconsin Press, Madison.

Enderson, J.H. and J. Craig. 1974. Status of the Peregrine Falcon in the Rocky Mountains in 1973. The Auk 91: 727-736.

Enderson, J.H., W. Heinrich, L. Kiff, and C.M. White. 1995. Population changes in North American peregrines. Transactions of the North American Wildlife and Natural Resources Conference 60:142-161.

Fuller, M.R. and J.A. Mosher. 1987. Raptor survey techniques. Pp. 37-66 *In* Raptor management techniques manual. B.A.G. Pendleton, B.A. Millsap, K.W. Cline, and D.W. Bird, eds. Natl. Wildl. Fed., Washington, D.C.

Fyfe, R.W., U. Banasch, V. Benavides, N.H. de Benavides, A. Luscombe, and J. Sanchez. 1990. Organochlorine residues in potential prey of peregrine falcons, *Falco peregrinus*, in Latin America. Can. Field-Nat. 104(2):285–292.

Gilbertson, M., T. Kubiak, J. Ludwig, and G. Fox. 1991. Great Lakes embryo mortality, edema, and deformities syndrome (GLEMEDS) in colonial fish-eating birds: similarity to chick-edema disease. J. Toxicol. Environ. Health 33:455-520.

Hayes, G.E., and J.B. Buchanan. 2002. Washington State status report for the Peregrine Falcon. Washington Dept. Fish and Wildlife, Olympia. 77 pp.

Henny, C.J., W.S. Seegar, and T.L. Maechtle. 1996. DDT decreases in plasma of spring migrant peregrine falcons, 1978–94. J. Wildl. Manage. 60:342–349.

Herbert, R.A., and K.G.S. Herbert. 1969. The extirpation of the Hudson River Peregrine Falcon population. Pp. 133-154 *In* Peregrine Falcon populations: their biology and decline. J.J. Hickey, ed. Univ. of Wisconsin Press, Madison.

Hickey, J.J. 1942. Eastern population of the Duck Hawk. Auk 59:176-204.

Hickey, J.J. and D.W. Anderson. 1968. Chlorinated hydrocarbons and eggshell changes in raptorial and fish-eating birds. Science 162:271-273.

Hickey, J.J. and D.W. Anderson. 1969. The peregrine falcon: life history and population literature. Pp. 3-42 *In* Peregrine falcon populations: their biology and decline. J.J. Hickey, ed. University of Wisconsin Press, Madison, Wisconsin.

Hunt, W.G. 1998. Raptor floaters at Moffat's equilibrium. Oikos 82: 191-197.

Jarman, W.M. 1994. Levels and trends of DDE in California peregrines. U.S. Fish and Wildlife Service Report. 16 pp.

Johnstone, R.M., G.S. Court, A.C. Fesser, D.M. Bradley, L.W. Oliphant, and J.D. MacNeil. 1996. Long-term trends and sources of organochlorine contamination in Canadian tundra Peregrine Falcons, *Falco peregrinus tundrius*. Environmental Pollution. 93(2): 109-120.

Kiff, L.F. 1988. Changes in the status of the Peregrine in North America: An overview. Pp. 123-139 *In* Peregrine falcon populations: their management and recovery. T.J. Cade, J.H. Enderson, C.G. Thelander, and C.M. White, eds. The Peregrine Fund, Boise, Idaho.

Mesta, R. 1999. Final Rule to Remove the American Peregrine Falcon from the Federal list of endangered and threatened wildlife, and to remove the similarity of appearance provision for free-flying peregrines in the conterminous United States. Federal Register 64 (164): 46541-46558.

Mora, M., R. Skiles, B. McKinney, M. Paredes, D. Buckler, D. Papoulias, and D. Klein. 2002. Environmental contaminants in prey and tissues of the peregrine falcon in the Big Bend Region, Texas, USA. Environmental Pollution 116:169-176.

Morse, N.J. 1994. Contaminants in peregrine falcon (*Falco peregrinus*) eggs from Virginia, Maryland, and West Virginia. Technical Report, U.S. Fish and Wildlife Service, Virginia Field Office, White Marsh, VA. 19 pp.

Pagel, J.E. 1992. Protocol for observing known and potential peregrine falcon eyries in the Pacific Northwest. Pp. 83-96 *In* Proceedings: Symposium on peregrine falcons in the Pacific Northwest. J.E. Pagel, ed. Rogue River National Forest, Medford, OR 97501.

Peakall, D.B., D.G. Noble, J.E. Elliott, J.D. Somers, and G. Erickson. 1990. Environmental contaminants in Canadian peregrine falcons, *Falco peregrinus*: A toxicological assessment. Can. Field-Nat. 104:244-254.

Powell, D.C., R.J. Aulerich, R.J. Balander, K.L. Stromborg, and S.J. Bursian. 1998. A photographic guide to the development of double-crested cormorant embryos. Colonial Waterbirds 21(3):348-355.

Ratcliffe, D. 1993. The Peregrine Falcon, 2nd ed. T. & A.D. Poyser, London. 454 pp.

Rowell, P., G.L. Holroyd, and U. Banasch. 2003. Summary of the 2000 Canadian peregrine falcon survey. Bird Trends, No. 9, Raptors (Winter 2003):52-56. Canadian Wildlife Service, http://www.cws-scf.ec.gc.ca/birds/news/index_e.cfm

Steenhof, K. 1987. Assessing raptor reproductive success and productivity. p. 157-170 *In* Raptor management techniques manual. B.A.G. Pendleton, B.A. Millsap, K.W. Cline, and D.W. Bird, eds. Natl. Wildl. Fed., Washington, D.C.

Steidl, R.J., C.R. Griffin, L.J. Niles, and K.E. Clark. 1991. Reproductive success and eggshell thinning of a reestablished peregrine falcon population. J. Wildl. Manage. 55:294-299.

Steidl, R.J., J.P. Hayes, and E. Schauber. 1997. Statistical power in wildlife research. J. Wildl. Manage. 61:270-279.

Stickel, L.F., S.N. Wiemeyer, and L.J. Blus. 1973. Pesticide residues in eggs of wild birds: adjustment for loss of moisture and lipid. Bull. Environ. Contam. Toxicol. 9:193-196.

Tordoff, H.B. and P.T. Redig. 1997. Midwest peregrine falcon demography, 1982-1995. J. Raptor Res. 31: 339-346.

U.S. Fish and Wildlife Service. 1982a. Recovery plan for the peregrine falcon -- Alaska population. 69 pp.

U.S. Fish and Wildlife Service. 1982b. The Pacific Coast American peregrine falcon recovery plan, dated October 12, 1982, prepared by the U.S. Fish and Wildlife Service in cooperation with Pacific Coast American Peregrine Falcon Recovery Team. 86 pp.

U.S. Fish and Wildlife Service. 1984. American peregrine falcon recovery plan (Rocky Mountain/Southwest population). Prepared in cooperation with the American Peregrine Falcon Recovery Team. U.S. Fish and Wildlife Service, Denver, CO. 105 pp.

U.S. Fish and Wildlife Service. 1991. First update of peregrine falcon (*Falco peregrinus*), eastern population, revised recovery plan. Newton Corner, MA. 35 pp.

U.S. Fish and Wildlife Service. 1994. Contaminants in Peregrine Falcon (*Falco peregrinus*) eggs from Virginia, Maryland, and West Virginia. Virginia Field Office. Pleasantville, New Jersey. 19pp.

U.S. Fish and Wildlife Service. 1995. Recovery plan for the Mexican spotted owl: Vol.I. Albuquerque, New Mexico. 172pp.

U.S. Fish and Wildlife Service and New Jersey Department of Environmental Protection. 1997. Draft report, reproductive success and egg contaminant concentrations of Southern New Jersey peregrine falcons. 34 pp.

White, C.M., N.J. Clum, T.J. Cade, and W.G. Hunt. 2002. Peregrine Falcon (*Falco peregrinus*). *In* The Birds of North America, No. 660. A. Poole and F. Gill, eds. The Birds of North America, Inc., Philadelphia, PA.

Figure 1: FWS, Recovery, and Monitoring Regions.
bold

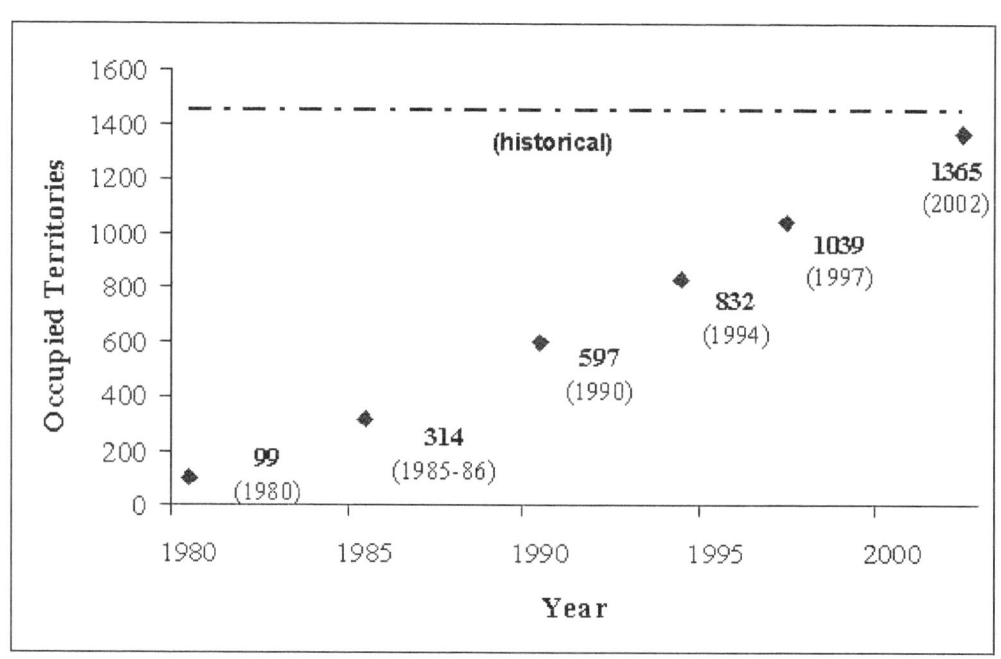

Figure 2. Peregrine Population Growth, 1980-2002, in the Contiguous United States. Historical data from Enderson et al. (1995) and Mesta (1999). More recent data collected from cooperators (FWS, unpubl.). 2002 data includes estimates, earlier data are counts. North American population, including Mexico, Canada, and Alaska, estimated at nearly 3,000 breeding pairs in 2002 (White et al. 2002; Rowell et al. 2003; FWS unpubl. data). Historical level in the United States south of Canada roughly estimated at 1,450 pairs (interpreted from Enderson et al. 1995).

27

Appendix A: Authors, National and Regional Coordinators

National Coordinator

Mike Green
USFWS, Region 1, Migratory Birds and Habitat Programs
911 N.E. 11th Ave.
Portland, OR 97232-4181
Tel. (503) 872 - 2707
Fax (503) 231 - 2019

Regional Coordinators

Region 1 – California, Hawaii, Idaho, Nevada, Oregon, Pacific Islands, Washington
Marie Morin
USFWS, Ecological Services
Oregon State Office
2600 S.E. 98th Ave., Suite 100
Portland, Oregon 97266
Tel. (503) 231 - 6179
Fax (503) 231 - 6195

Region 2 – Arizona, New Mexico, Oklahoma, Texas.
Robert Mesta, Coordinator
Sonoran Joint Venture
738, N. Fifth Ave. Ste 215
Tucson, Arizona 85705
Tel. (520) 882 - 0047
Fax (520) 882 - 0370
Cell (520) 591-4566

Region 3 – Illinois, Indiana, Iowa, Michigan, Minnesota, Missouri, Ohio, Wisconsin.
Phil Delphey
USFWS, Ecological Services
Twin Cities Field Office
4101 E. 80th St.
Bloomington, Minnesota 55425
Tel. (612) 725 - 3548 x 206
Fax (612) 725 - 3609

Region 4 – Alabama, Arkansas, Florida, Georgia, Kentucky, Louisiana, Mississippi, North Carolina, South Carolina, Tennessee, Virgin Islands, Puerto Rico.
Robert Currie
USFWS, Ecological Services
Asheville Field Office
160 Zillicoa St.
Asheville, North Carolina 28801
Tel. (828) 258 - 3939 ext. 224
Fax (828) 258 - 5330

Region 5 – Connecticut, District of Columbia, Delaware, Maine, Maryland, Massachusetts, New Hampshire, New Jersey, New York, Pennsylvania, Rhode Island, Vermont, Virginia, West Virginia.
Michael Amaral
USFWS, Ecological Services
New England Field Office
70 Commercial St., Ste. 300
Concord, New Hampshire 03301-4986
Tel. (603) 223 - 2541
Fax (603) 223 - 0104

Region 6 – Colorado, Kansas, Montana, Nebraska, North Dakota, South Dakota, Utah, Wyoming.
Rob Hazlewood
USFWS, Ecological Services
Montana Field Office
100 North Park, Suite 320
Helena, Montana 59604
Tel. (406) 449 - 5225 ext. 211
Fax (406) 449 -5339

Region 7 – Alaska
Ted Swem
USFWS, Fairbanks Fish and Wildlife Office
101 12th Ave., Box 19
Fairbanks, Alaska 99501
Tel. (907) 456 - 0441
Fax (907) 456 - 0208

Additional Authors
Kathy Hollar
USFWS, Region 1, Endangered Species
911 N.E. 11th Ave.
Portland, OR 97232-4181
Tel. (503) 231 - 2359
Fax (503) 231 - 6243

Martin Miller and Mary Klee
USFWS, Division of HCPs, Recovery, and State Grants
4401 N. Fairfax Dr.
Mail Stop 420 Arlington Square
Arlington, VA 22203
Tel. (703) 358 - 2061
Fax (703) 358 - 1735

Angela Matz
USFWS, Fairbanks Fish and Wildlife Office
101 12th Ave., Box 19
Fairbanks, Alaska 99501
Tel. (907) 456 - 0442
Fax (907) 456 - 0208

Appendix B: Reviewers and Cooperators

Name	Affiliation	Address
	FWS Region 1	
Jennifer Brookshier	WA Dept. of Fish and Wildlife	600 Capitol Way North, Olympia, WA 98501
Charlie Bruce	OR Dept. of Fish and Wildlife	2501 SW First Avenue, P.O. Box 59, Portland, OR 97207
Eric Cummins	WA Dept. of Fish and Wildlife	600 Capitol Way North, Olympia, WA 98501
Janet Linthicum	Santa Cruz Predatory Bird Research Group, Long Marine Laboratory	100 Shaffer Road, Santa Cruz, CA 95060
Joel Pagel	USFS, Rogue River National Forest	645 Washington St., Ashland, OR 97520
Rex Sallabanks, Ph.D.	Idaho Department of Fish and Game	600 South Walnut, P.O. Box 25, Boise, Idaho 83707-0025
Cris Tomlinson	Nevada Div. of Wildlife	4747 W. Vegas Drive, Las Vegas, Nevada 89108
Brian Walton	Santa Cruz Predatory Bird Research Group, Long Marine Laboratory	100 Shaffer Road, Santa Cruz, CA 95060
Bryan White	OR Dept. of Fish and Wildlife	7118 NE Vandenberg Ave, Corvallis, OR 97330
	FWS Region 2	
Fred Armstrong	NPS, Guadalupe Mountains National Park	HC 60 Box 400, Salt Flat, Texas 79847
Larry Bell	Department of Game and Fish	1 Wildlife Way, P.O. Box 25112, Santa Fe, NM 87504
Elaine Leslie	Grand Canyon National Park, NPS	P.O. Box 129, Grand Canyon NP, AZ 86023
Robert Magill	AZ Game & Fish Dept.	2221 W. Greenway Road, Phoenix, AZ 85023
Raymond Skiles	NPS, Big Bend National Park	P.O. Box 129, Big Bend National Park, TX 79834
Robert Steidl, Ph.D.	School of Renewable Resources, University of AZ	325 Biol. Sciences East, Tuscon, AZ 85721

31

Name	Affiliation	Address
Sandy Williams	Department of Game and Fish	1 Wildlife Way, P.O. Box 25112, Santa Fe, NM 87504
FWS Region 3		
John Castrale	Indiana Division of Fish and Wildlife	562 DNR Rd., Mitchell, IN 47446
Mike Cooke	World Bird Sanctuary	P.O. Box 270270, St. Louis, Missouri 63127
Mary Hennen	Field Museum of Natural History	1400 S. Lake Shore Drive, Chicago, IL 60605
Tara Kieninger	Department of Natural Resources	524 South 2nd St., Springfield, IL 62701
Pat Manthey	Department of Natural Resources	3550 Mormon Coulee Rd., La Crosse WI 54601
Mark Martell	The Raptor Center	Gabbert Raptor Building, 1920 Fitch Ave. St. Paul, MN, 55108
Lee Pfannmuller	Minnesota Dept. of Natural Resources	500 Lafayette Rd., St. paul, MN 55155-4025 MI
Ray Rustum		
Pat Schlarbaum	Boone Wildlife Research Station	2039 205th St., Boone, Iowa 50036
Dave Scott	Division of Wildlife	8589 Horseshoe Rd., Ashley, OH 43003
Bud Tordoff	The Raptor Center	Gabbert Raptor Building, 1920 Fitch Ave. St. Paul, MN, 55108
FWS Region 4		
Mary Bunch	South Carolina Department of Natural Resources	PO Box 1806, Clemson, SC 29633
Kim Delozier	Great Smoky Mountains NP	107 Park Headquarters Road, Gatlinburg, TN 37738
Roy DeWitt	Georgia Falconry Association	993 Camillia Dr., Marietta, GA 30062
Troy Ettel	Tennessee Wildlife Resources Agency	Ellington Agricultural Center, PO Box 40747, Nashville, TN 37204
Chris McGrath	North Carolina Wildlife Resources Commission	315 Morgan Branch Rd.,Leicester, NC 28748
Jim Ozier	Georgia Department of Natural Resources	116 Rum Creek Drive, Forsyth, GA 31029
Brainard Palmer-Ball	Kentucky State Nature Preserves Commission	801 Schenkel Lane, Frankfort, KY 40601
Tim Slone	Kentucky Department of Fish and	1 Game Farm Rd., Frankfort, KY 40601

Name	Affiliation	Address
Jim Sorrow	Wildlife Resources South Carolina Department of Natural Resources	4037 India Hook Rd., Rock Hill, SC 29732
Shawchyi Vorisek	Kentucky Department of Fish and Wildlife Resources	1 Game Farm Rd., Frankfort, KY 40601
FWS Region 5		
Daniel Brauning	Penn. Game Commission	61 Windy Lane, Montgomery, PA 17752
Kathy Clark	NJ Dept. of Fish, Game and Wildlife	Tuckahoe Wildlife Mgmt. Area, Box 236, Tuckahoe, NJ 08250
Margaret Fowle	National Wildlife Federation	Northeastern Natural Resource Center, 58 State St, Montpelier, VT 05602
Tom French	Massachusetts Division of Fisheries and Wildlife	Route 135, Westborough, MA 01581
Craig Koppie	FWS, Chesapeake Bay Field Office	177 Admiral Cochrane Dr., Annapolis, MD 21401
Barbara Loucks	NY State Dept. of Environmental Conservation	625 Broadway, Albany, NY 12233
Chris Martin	Audubon Society of New Hampshire	3 Silk Farm Road, Concord, NH 03301
Holly Niederriter	DNREC, Division of Fish and Wildlife	4876 Hay Point Landing Road, Smyrna, DE 19977
Mark Stadler	Wildlife Division, Dept. of Inland Fisheries and Wildlife	284 State St., Augusta, ME 04333
Charlie Todd	Maine Dept. Inland Fisheries & Wildlife	284 State St., 41 State House Station, Augusta, ME 04333-0041
Julie Victoria	Dept. of Environmental Conservation	Franklin Wildlife Management Area, 391 Rte. 32, North Franklin, CT 05254
Bryan Watts	William and Mary College	The Center for Conservation Biology, College of William & Mary, PO Box 8795, Williamsburg, VA 23187-8795
FWS Region 6		
Jerry Craig	Colorado Division of Wildlife	6060 Broadway, Denver, Colorado 80216
Frank Howe	Utah Division of Wildlife	P.O. Box 146301, Salt Lake City, UT 84114

33

Name	Affiliation	Address
Bob Oakleaf	Wyoming Game and Fish Department	260 Buena Vista, Lander, WY 82520
Jay Sumner	Sumner Consulting	P.O. Box 317, Arlee, MT 59821
FWS Region 7		
Skip Ambrose	NPS	Natural Sounds Program, National Park Service, 1201 Oakridge, Suite 200, Fort Collins, CO 80525
Bob Ritchie	ABR, Inc.	P.O. Box 80410, Fairbanks, AK 99708
John Wright	Alaska Department of Fish and Game	Division of Wildlife Conservation, 1300 College Rd, Fairbanks, AK 99701

Appendix C: Sample Peregrine Falcon Monitoring Form

----- Return this form to your State or Regional Coordinator ----

Observation Date:(M/D/YR)_____   Nest Site Name or #_____
Which Territory Visit is this? (circle one)   1st   2nd   3rd   4th
Nest Site (circle one):   Manmade   Natural
Observation Time: Begin_____ End_____
(Should be at least 4 hrs if occupancy, nest age, or nestling number are in question)

Observer(s)_____

Phone:_____ Email:_____ Agency/NGO_____

WEATHER: Precipitation_____ Wind (speed estimate)_____

          Temperature_____ Cloud cover (%)_____
          Note conditions at beginning (beg.) and ending (end) of observation period if different

Observation post:(distance in meters)_____

Approx. Nesting Phase (determined how?)_____
_____

Peregrines present: (define as ad. male, ad. female, ad. unknown, subad. Male, subad. Female, or subad. Unknown, and number of each.)_____

Behaviors observed:_____
_____
_____
_____

Nest observed? Y N   Feeding at nest observed? Y N   Eggs observed? Y N Unk
How many eggs?_____ Young observed (AGE)?_____
How many young?_____ Other observations:_____
_____
_____
_____
_____
_____
_____
_____
_____
_____
_____
_____
_____

Occupied Territory - a territory where either a pair of Peregrines is present (two adults or an adult/subadult mixed pair), or there is evidence of reproduction [e.g., one adult is observed sitting low in the nest, eggs or young are seen, or food is delivered into eyrie (nest site)]. Occupancy for a territory must be established for at least one of two, and possibly more, 4-hour site visits. Occupancy within a region is the number of occupied territories divided by the number of territories that were checked for occupancy.

Nest Success - the proportion of occupied territories in a monitoring region in which one or more young ≥ 28 days old is observed, with age determined following guidelines in Cade et al. (1996).

Productivity - the number of young observed at ≥ 28 days old per occupied territory, averaged across a monitoring region.

Paperwork Reduction Act: The total annual public reporting burden for gathering information under this Peregrine Falcon monitoring plan is estimated to be 190 hours in 2002, 220 hours in 2003, and 270 hours in 2004. This includes time for reviewing instructions, gathering and maintaining data, and preparing and transmitting reports. Comments regarding the burden estimate or any other aspect of the reporting requirement(s) should be directed to the Service Information Collection Clearance Officer, MS 222 ARL SQ, Fish and Wildlife Service, 1849 C Street NW, Washington, DC 20240.

An agency may not conduct and a person is not required to respond to a collection of information unless a currently valid OMB control number is displayed.

Appendix D: FWS Regions, Recovery Plan Regions, and Monitoring Plan Regions

FWS Regions (7)	Recovery Regions[1] (4)	Monitoring Regions (6)
Region 1 = CA, ID, NV, OR, WA, HI, Guam, American Samoa, Commonwealth of the Northern Marianas	Pacific: CA, NV, OR, WA	Pacific: CA, ID, NV, OR, WA
Region 3 = IL, IN, IA, MI, MN, MO, OH, WI	Eastern: all of CT, DE, MA, ME, MI, MN, NH, NJ, NY, PA, RI, VT, WI, and Wash DC; parts of IA, IL, IN, OH, WV, MD, VA, NC, SC, AL, TN, and KY	Midwestern/Northeastern: IL, IN, IA, MI, MN, MO, OH, WI, CT, DE, ME, MD, MA, NH, NJ, NY, PA, RI, VT, VA, WV, and Wash DC
Region 5 = CT, DE, ME, MD, MA, NH, NJ, NY, PA, RI, VT, VA, WV, and Wash DC		
Region 4 = AL, AR, FL, GA, KY, LA, MS, NC, PR, SC, TN, VI		Southeastern: AL, AR, FL, GA, KY, LA, MS, NC, SC, TN
Region 2 = AZ, NM, OK, TX	Rocky Mts./Southwest: FWS Regions 2 and 6 Rocky Mts./Southwest Region (plus ID)	Southwestern: AZ, NM, OK, TX
Region 6 = CO, KS, MT, ND, NE, SD, UT, WY		Rocky Mountains: CO, KS, MT, ND, NE, SD, UT, WY
Region 7 = AK	Alaska	Alaska

1 – Recovery regions are for the American Peregrine Falcon only; recovery areas vary for each listed species.

Appendix E: FWS Region Territory Summaries

Most data are from 1999 - 2002. Exceptions are noted in parentheses.

State by FWS Region	Territories Occupied ≥ 1 time in '99-'02[†]	Natural Nest substrate	Man-made substrate	Data Source[‡]
FWS Region 1				
California	96	77	19	Brian Walton & Janet Linthicum
Idaho	24 (to year 2001)	22	2	Rex Sallabanks
Nevada	12	12		Cris Tomlinson
Oregon	97	93	4	Joel Pagel, Charlie Bruce, & Bryan White
Washington	81 (to year 2001)	73	8	Eric Cummins & Jennifer Brookshier
R1 Totals	310	≥ 277	≥ 33	
FWS Region 2				
Arizona (in 1997)	172	?	?	Robert Magill & Elaine Leslie
New Mexico	101	?	?	Sandy Williams
Texas**	14	14	0	Missy Paul, Raymond Skiles, & Fred Armstrong
R2 Totals	287	≥ 14	?	
FWS Region 3				
Iowa	5	1	4	Pat Schlarbaum
Illinois	10	0	10	Mary Hennen, Tara Kieninger, Bud Tordoff, & Mark Martell

State by FWS Region	Territories Occupied ≥ 1 time in '99-'02[†]	Natural Nest substrate	Man-made substrate	Data Source[‡]
Indiana	10	0	10	John Castrale, Bud Tordoff, & Mark Martell
Michigan	7	1	6	Bud Tordoff, Mark Martell, & Ray Rustem
Minnesota	27	7	20	Bud Tordoff & Mark Martell
Missouri	6	0	6	Mike Cooke, Bud Tordoff, & Mark Martell
Ohio	14	0	14	Dave Scott, Bud Tordoff, & Mark Martell
Wisconsin	17	2	15	Pat Manthey, Bud Tordoff, & Mark Martell
R3 Totals	96	11	85	
FWS Region 4				
Georgia	1	0	1	Jim Ozier
Kentucky	4	0	4	Tim Slone & Shawchyi Vorisek
North Carolina	10	10	0	Chris McGrath
South Carolina	1	1	0	Bob Currie & Mary Bunch
Tennessee	2	1	1	Troy Ettel
R4 Totals	18	12	6	
FWS Region 5				
Connecticut	4	1	3	Julie Victoria
Delaware	4	0	4	Holly Niederriter & Craig Koppie
Massachusetts	8	1	7	Tom French

39

State by FWS Region	Territories Occupied ≥ 1 time in '99-'02[†]	Natural Nest substrate	Man-made substrate	Data Source[‡]
Maine	16	16	0	Charlie Todd
Maryland	13	?	?	Craig Koppie & Michael Amaral
New Hampshire	15	14	1	Chris Martin
New Jersey	21	1	20	Kathy Clark
New York	52	32	20	Barbara Loucks
Pennsylvania	9	0	9	Daniel Brauning
Rhode Island	2	0	2	Michael Amaral
Virginia	29	2	27	Bryan Watts, W. & Mary College
Vermont	31	29	2*	Margaret Fowle
R5 Totals	204	≥ 96	≥ 95	
FWS Region 6				
Colorado	132	132	?	Jerry Craig
Montana	43 (to year 2001)	?	?	Jay Sumner
Nebraska	1		1	Bud Tordoff
North Dakota	1		1	Bud Tordoff
Utah	180	168	12	Frank Howe
Wyoming	62	62	0	Bob Oakleaf
R6 Totals	419	≥ 362	≥ 14	

40

State by FWS Region	Territories Occupied ≥ 1 time in '99-'02[†]	Natural Nest substrate	Man-made substrate	Data Source[‡]
FWS Region 7				
AK-Tanana River	≥ 44	44	0	Bob Ritchie, John Wright, and Peter Bente
AK-Yukon River	≥ 48	48	0	Skip Ambrose
R7 Totals	≥ 92	≥ 92	0	
40 States	$\geq$ **1,426**	$\geq$ **771**	$\geq$**232**	

Of 1093 categorized sites, 864 (79%) were on natural substrates and 232 (21%) were on man-made sites; uncategorized sites are likely on natural substrates in Arizona and New Mexico.

† – Number of territories occupied is a subset of the total population in some western States, e.g., in Alaska and California.
‡ – Affiliations and addresses of those supplying data are listed in Appendix B.
* – These 2 are in a quarry and road cut.
** – Information from Big Bend and Guadalupe National Parks only.
? – Unknown, or data not provided.

Appendix F: Calculating Territory Occupancy and Nest Success

The calculations of territory occupancy and nest success are used for two purposes: to help define the appropriate sample size, and to provide benchmarks by which to compare future population performance. The data from which we calculated these rates are described in more detail below.

Territory Occupancy

Table F-1 shows rates of occupancy at territories occupied at least once between 1999 and 2002. Data from the 4 years are combined, and some data (FWS Regions 1 and 2) are from 1997. Occupied territories are those at which there was a pair of Peregrines, or evidence of nesting (see the Methods - Parameters and Definitions section, above).

Table F-1. Territory Occupancy 1999-2002

FWS Region	Checked	Occupied	Average
1	860	738	0.86
2	305	229	0.75
3	231	214	0.93
4	90	84	0.93
5	720	580	0.81
6	735	608	0.83
7	33	31	0.94
All n	2974	2484	0.84

Nest Success

The data in Table F-2 are the same as above, except that 'Occupied' territories includes territories found after initiation (and then were checked again for success); the sample size is therefore different from the 'Occupied' sample above. States were asked to define successful nests as those from which at least one chick fledged. Some consider chicks of banding age to meet this criterion. We accepted this definition for these data.

Table F-2. Nest Success, 1999-2002

FWS Region	Occupied	Successful	Mean
1	640	446	0.70
2	212	144	0.68
3	214	156	0.73
4	82	50	0.61
5	198	136	0.69
6	812	555	0.68
7	421	269	0.64
All n	2579	1756	0.68

A Note on Territory Occupancy

This statistic is sensitive to what sort of territory is actually being checked. In some states (principally in Region 5) many historical eyries continue to be checked although they have not been occupied for decades, while in others only more recently occupied territories are checked for activity. In the tables above, we chose to use only territories that have been used at least once since 1999 (1997 for some western states without more recent data) to represent current and likely future conditions under which Peregrines make territory choices. Some historical eyries or territories that remain unoccupied might not be as attractive as they once were, for many reasons, than newer, more recently occupied territories. Including historical and unoccupied territories in this analysis brings the national average to 77% (and Region 5 average to 51%).

Also, in this plan we will be collecting territory occupancy data from this same 'population' of territories. The data we collect will be directly comparable to the rates calculated above, which we think are representative of a healthy, expanding population. However, additional data are worth noting here.

Territory occupancy for 1999 to 2002 was similar during the critical years of recovery. For example, data from western states from 1975 (California) to 1997 are presented in Table F-3 below; these include only territories known to have been occupied at least once in the interval noted.

Table F-3. Territory Occupancy in Western States, 1975-1997

FWS Region	State (yr)	Checked	Occupied	Average
R1	CA (75 - 97)	147	111	0.76
R1	WA (78 - 97)	401	298	0.74
R2	AZ (92 - 97)	297	265	0.89
R2	TX (79 - 94)	83	67	0.81
R6	CO (90 - 95, 97)	549	444	0.81
R6	MT (1995)	19	15	0.79
R6	UT (91 - 96)	514	465	0.91
R6	WY (96)	38	36	0.95
	All n	2048	1701	0.83

Most of these data were acquired by Robert Mesta in 1998 in preparation for the Peregrine delisting, from the following cooperators: Santa Cruz Predatory Bird Research Group; Arizona Game and Fish Department; Texas Parks and Wildlife Department; the southwest Peregrine recovery team; Utah Division of Wildlife Resources; the National Park Service. Data also from Hayes and Buchanan (2002; full cite in Literature Cited section of plan). All data believed to conform to definitions of occupancy used in this plan, and are likely lower than actual occupancy for some states, e.g., in CA.

Territory occupancy is 83% summing western states, ranging from 74% to 95% for individual states. Nationwide territory occupancy from 1999 - 2002 (Table F-1) is 84%, ranging from 75% to 94%, and thus is very similar. These data are also similar to published rates. Enderson and Craig (1974) state that "at least 10%, perhaps 20%, of known eyries would not be used in any one year (p 733)," after citing various published rates of territory occupancy that averaged between 55% and 85%. Ratcliffe (1993) estimates territory occupancy at 82 % in 1991 (Table 6, p. 411) for Peregrines in Great Britain.

Some Peregrine eyries are famous for their long histories of occupancy; others are much less consistently occupied. Some pairs or individuals select alternate nest sites sometimes miles apart within a larger territory in successive years, or move erratically back and forth among a few eyrie locations among years. Some territories are seemingly occupied only once and then abandoned. Observers in the field are thus challenged to find active territories in the first place, locate nests in those territories, and then to relocate the same pairs and nests in following years. Where several pairs are in close proximity, tracking pair locations through time and deciding which territories and pairs are new or previously established can be confusing. In these cases, we will rely on the expert opinions of observers to match previously documented territories to current pair and territory locations.

Appendix G: Collecting, Preparing, and Shipping Egg and Feather Samples

All sample collectors should coordinator with Regional and National Coordinators prior to collection and if additional information is required.

A. Protocol for Collection and Removal of Peregrine Egg Contents

Objectives
1. Ensure accurate analysis of contaminants in eggs by providing standard methods to transfer egg contents from the shell into a clean container without introducing contamination.

2. Provide a standard method to measure eggshell thickness.

Materials
For field collection: Appropriate State and Federal permits; writing utensils; labels; egg collection boxes (hard-sided container such as plastic kitchen ware or tackle box with foam padding); sheets of chemically-clean[2] aluminum foil, cut to size (approximately 10 x 15 cm), one per egg; small plastic bags with zip closure.

For contents removal in laboratory: Data sheets; writing utensils; safety glasses; powder-free latex gloves; laboratory paper wipes such as Kimwipes®; distilled, deionized (DD) water or equivalently pure water; clean sponge; balance (to 0.01 g); vernier calipers (to 0.01 mm); immersion chamber with beaker and wire loops (Figure G-1); Teflon® bags, one per egg; chemically-clean stainless steel serrated blades (such as high-quality steak knives); chemically-clean stainless steel scalpel blades (No. 21 or No. 22 with No. 4 handles or similar size); chemically-clean aluminum foil sheets (approximately 30 x 30 cm square), 1 per egg; ball-tip micrometer (to 0.01 mm).

Procedures
In the field, collect all whole, uncracked, addled eggs from nest. Wrap each in clean aluminum foil (dull side next to the egg). The foil should act as a second skin, which keeps the eggshell together and the contents inside should the egg be cracked in transit. Place the wrapped egg inside bag with zip closure, then into hard container for transport to refrigeration (within 24 hours). Use padding to immobilize the egg. Place a label inside the zip-closure bag with date, collector, nest identification and location (latitude

---

2 — Chemically-clean aluminum foil has been rinsed with reagent-grade acetone and hexanes on the dull side and allowed to air-dry; dull side is then considered the "clean" side. Chemically-clean stainless instruments are rinsed with 10-20% nitric acid, then doubly-distilled or equivalently purified water, air-dried, then rinsed with reagent-grade acetone and hexanes and air-dried.

and longitude or UTM coordinates), and the egg number if multiple eggs are collected. Refrigerate eggs until opened (ideally within 48 hours).

In the laboratory, use one data form (Figure G-2) per egg. Wear powder-free latex gloves and safety glasses (severe eye infection can result from contact with rotting egg contents). Carefully check for cracks in shell; if present, do not wet or immerse the egg. If debris is present, rinse egg in DD water while gently scrubbing with sponge. Dry the egg. Record the mass (g) of the whole egg, then measure the length and breadth of the egg at their greatest dimensions with calipers (caliper jaws parallel to the longitudinal axis of the egg for length, perpendicular to the longitudinal axis of the egg for breadth). Compute average of three measurements for final width and length measurements.

Measure total egg volume by water displacement. Fill the immersion chamber (Figure G-1a) with distilled water past the point where water comes out of the spigot. Let drain until water stops coming out of the spigot. Place a clean beaker on a balance, zero the balance, and place the balance and beaker under the spigot (Figure G-1b). Immerse egg with wire loops (Figure G-1c) until top of egg is just under the water surface. Hold the egg steady until water stops draining out of spigot into the beaker. The readout on the balance will reflect only the weight of water that has gone into the beaker, if you zeroed the balance after the beaker was placed on it. The weight of water is the approximate egg volume, assuming that egg density is similar to water (1gm = 1 ml). For example, 40 gm displaced water = 40 ml of water, and 40 ml egg volume. Dry the egg.

While transferring egg contents to Teflon® bag, avoid letting contents run over your hands into the bag. Note that addled eggs can be full of decomposition products, producing gaseous explosions at any weak point in the shell, including the score or where membranes are first exposed. Working with a refrigerated, cool egg reduces this potential, but be prepared for egg explosions – and wear safety glasses.

Create a catch basin out of the aluminum foil (chemically-clean side up) by turning edges up and securing the corners. This will catch egg contents in case they spill over the edge of the bag. Use a separate piece of foil for each sample. The foil also is a clean place to place your instruments when they are not in use. Tare balance with Teflon® bag, then place bag in center of aluminum foil.

Score egg at the equator with a clean serrated blade or scalpel. Cradle the egg in one hand without squeezing too tightly, and gently score while rotating the egg. Many light strokes are preferable to a fewer deeper strokes, increasing the evenness of the score and decreasing the possibility of fractured eggshells. Continue to score until you see the membrane, which usually appears gray underneath the white of the eggshell. Try to expose the membrane evenly around the entire egg.

Place the egg over the open bag and cut through membranes with the scalpel. Pour contents into bag, and use the scalpel to gently scrape if necessary. Close the bag. Note where the membranes are, as this is important for thickness measurements. For fresh eggs, both membranes often stay with the shell, but as the embryo develops the inner

46

membrane tends to stick with the embryo. If you cannot determine where the membranes are, it often becomes clearer after the eggshell and membranes have dried. Record mass of full bag, then subtract tare mass to compute egg contents mass. Label the bag with nest and egg identification information. Freeze the sample (-40° C is preferable but 0° C is adequate) until shipment to central repository.

If egg is developed, estimate age of embryo. Peregrine incubation is 29-33 days (Ehrlich et al. 1988); estimate age of embryo to first, second, third, or fourth quarter. Photographic records of avian embryo development provide reference points to make this determination (e.g., Powell et al. 1998, Bird et al. 1984). Note amount of decay (no decay, slightly decayed, or rotten) and examine for deformities, particularly bill deformities such as crossed bills or lack of jaws, but also lack of skull bones, club feet, rotated ankles, or dwarfed appendages (Gilbertson et al. 1991).

Rinse the eggshell halves with cool water and allow to air dry. Using an ultra-fine tip marker or pencil, identify each shell half (with nest and egg information). Dry eggshells at room temperature for 10-30 days, or until they have attained a constant mass. Then, measure thickness at three points near the equator on each shell half using ball-tip micrometer. Note whether you measured the membranes, as museum specimen thickness measurements often include the membranes. Finally, record the mass of the dried eggshell (to 0.001 g). This information is also used to compare to museum specimens.

Compute conversion factor, as explained on the data sheet. Historically, contaminant concentrations were multiplied by this conversion factor to get volume-adjusted residue data (Stickel et al. 1973).

Shipping
Place frozen, bagged contents in a cooler with dry ice (know the labeling requirements of your shipping company for dry ice) for shipping. If you are unable to find dry ice, contact Paul Becker (information below) for shipping instructions. Send via overnight service to the central storage repository:

> National Institute of Standards and Technology
> Hollings Marine Laboratory
> 331 Ft. Johnson Rd.
> Charleston, SC 29412
> Attn: Peregrine Project
> Paul Becker or Rebecca Pugh
> (843) 762-8861
> paul.becker@noaa.gov

Notify the recipient by telephone prior to shipping, and try to ship on Monday, Tuesday, or Wednesday to avoid weekend delays.

B. Protocol for Collection of Peregrine Feathers

Objective
1. Ensure accurate and precise analysis of metallic contaminants in feathers by providing methods to collect similar feathers from same-age Peregrines.

Materials
Appropriate State and Federal permits; writing utensils; labels; Teflon® collection bags; clean stainless steel scissors.

To collect feathers, the largest nestling (which is often the nestling with the most advanced feather development) will be the only nestling sampled per nest. Remove up to the distal 1.5 cm of the 4th secondary wing feather, from one side only, using clean stainless steel scissors. Do not cut the follicle, which is vascularized and therefore prone to bleeding during feather development. Store the sample in a Teflon® (Saivellex, Inc. or equivalent) collection envelope provided by the National Coordinator. Fill out the feather collection data form (Figure G-3). Feathers samples can be frozen or stored at room temperature.

Shipping
Send feather samples to the central storage repository via overnight or otherwise guaranteed service. Notify the recipient by telephone prior to shipping:

> National Institute of Standards and Technology
> Hollings Marine Laboratory
> 331 Ft. Johnson Rd.
> Charleston, SC 29412
> Attn: Peregrine Project
> Paul Becker or Rebecca Pugh
> (843) 762-8861
> paul.becker@noaa.gov

Literature Cited – Appendix G

Please see Literature Cited section above.

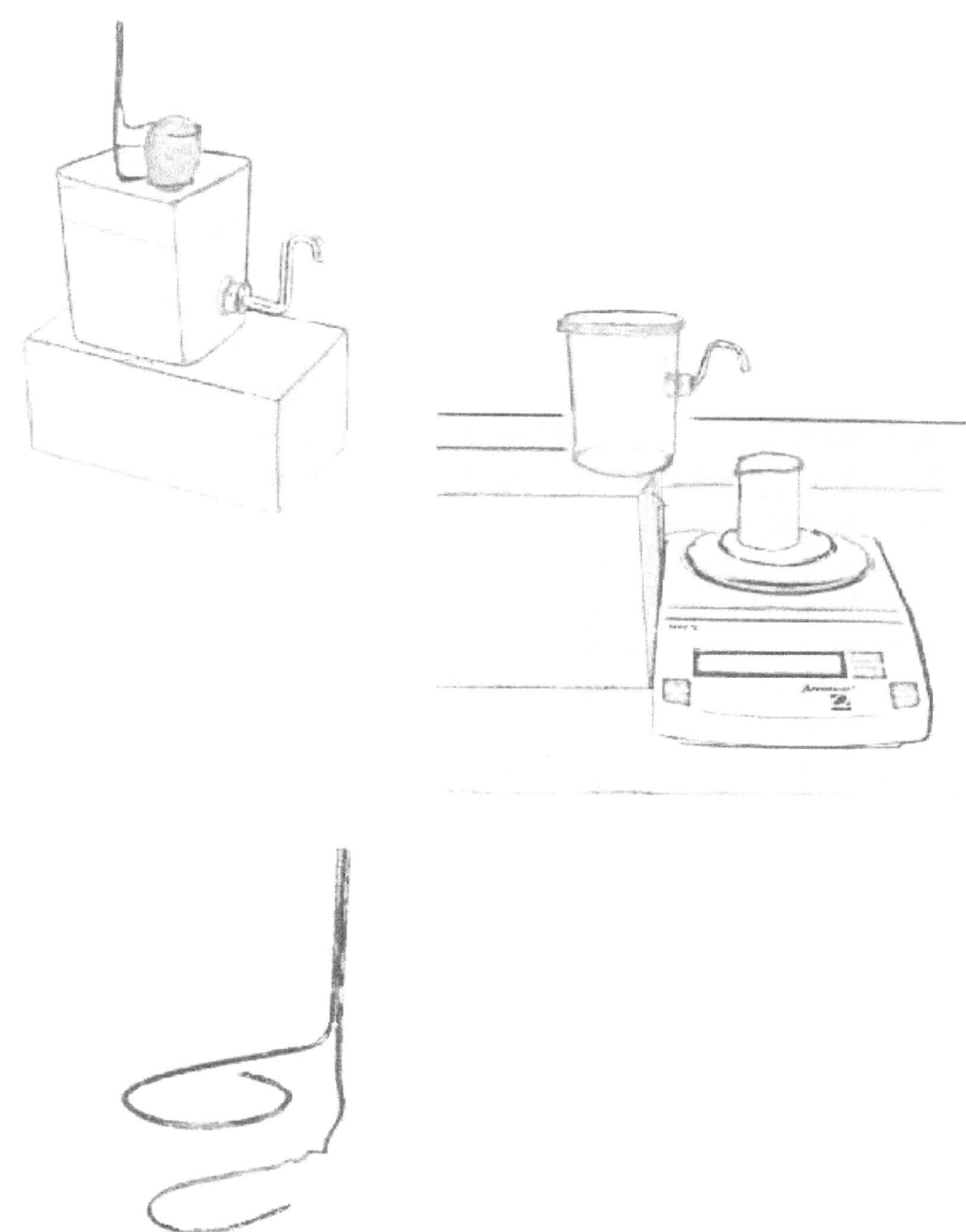

Figure G-1. Measuring Total Egg Volume.
the

Figure G-2. Peregrine Falcon Egg Contaminants Data Sheet

****
* Paperwork Reduction Act *
* OMB Approval No. 1018-0101 *
* Expires 3/31/2005 *
****

Monitoring Region: ______________________________

Collector name and affiliation: ______________________________

Processor name and affiliation: ______________________________

Date Collected: ______________ Date Processed: ______________

Nest Number or location:______________________________

Egg Number or description:______________________________

Nest status at time of collection:______________________________

(laying, incubating, abandoned, with chicks - how many, post-fledging, etc.)

Egg Length (three measurements, 0.1 mm):______ , ______ , ________ _______Average

Egg Width (three measurements, mm): _______ , _______ , ________ _______Average

Whole Egg Weight (0.01 g): _______

Weight of displaced H_2O (egg volume) (0.01 g): __________

Contents weight:

a) Tare weight of bag (0.01 g) : __________

b) Weight of bag plus contents (0.01 g): __________

c) Weight of contents (b-a): __________

Conversion factor = $\frac{\text{contents weight}}{\text{displaced } H_2O \text{ weight}}$ = ____________________

Contents condition (age of embryo, state of decay, etc.) and other comments:______________

____

____

Where are the membranes? Inner: ________________ Outer: ______________________

Eggshell thickness (0.01 mm) after > 10 days of air drying (note whether either, neither, or both membranes are included in the measurements):

First eggshell half: _____ ______ _____ _____ Avg: ______

Second eggshell half:_____ ______ _____ _____ Avg: ______ Overall Average: _______

Dry shell weight (mg) after > 10 days of air drying: __________________

Additional comments: ______________________________

____

____

____

____

Figure G-3. Peregrine Falcon Feather Contaminants Data Sheet

Monitoring Region: _____

Collector name and affiliation: _____

Date Collected: _____

Nest Number or location:_____

USFWS band number: _____

Additional band description and numbers: _____

Estimated age of nestling: _____

Estimated sex of nestling: _____

Was feather sample collected from (circle)   left   or   right   side of nestling?

Additional comments: _____
_____
_____
_____
_____
_____